To Amanda

handwritten inscription Diolch!

Gareth Writer-Davies

signature

Indigo Dreams Publishing

First Edition: Bodies
First published in Great Britain in 2015 by:
Indigo Dreams Publishing Ltd
24 Forest Houses
Halwill
Beaworthy
EX21 5UU
www.indigodreams.co.uk

Gareth Writer-Davies has asserted his right under the Copyright, Designs and Patents Act 1988 to be identified as the author of this work.
©2015 Gareth Writer-Davies

ISBN 978-1-909357-71-6

British Library Cataloguing in Publication Data. A CIP record for this book can be obtained from the British Library.

This book is sold subject to the condition that it shall not, by way of trade or otherwise, be lent, re-sold, hired out, or otherwise circulated without the author's and publisher's prior consent in any form of binding or cover other than that in which it is published and without a similar condition including this condition being imposed on the subsequent purchaser.

Designed and typeset in Palatino Linotype by Indigo Dreams.
Author photo by jadefindlater@flickr.com
Cover design by Ronnie Goodyer at Indigo Dreams.
Printed and bound in Great Britain by: 4edge Ltd.
www.4edge.co.uk
Papers used by Indigo Dreams are recyclable products made from wood grown in sustainable forests following the guidance of the Forest Stewardship Council.

To Cristina, without whom....

Thank you to Swarthmoor Hall, for the inspiration
and
David Van Cauter for editorial assistance.

Thanks are also due to the editors of The Journal and Ink, Sweat and Tears in which some of these poems first appeared.

"Bodies have their own light which they consume to live: they burn, they are not lit from the outside."
Egon Schiele

CONTENTS

- Fish 5
- Love 6
- Bone 7
- Ears 8
- Tortoise 9
- I Should Have Been Taller 10
- Little Weed 11
- My Heart 12
- The Slim Shape 13
- Breathe 14
- String 16
- Elbow 18
- Song Of The Hips 19
- Gut Flora 20
- Woman in her Bath 22
- Vertebrae 24
- Dental 25
- Hand 26
- The Claw 27
- Nose 28
- Ode To The Spleen 29
- Procedure 30
- Axilla 32
- Ambidextrous 33
- Bones 34

Fish

there was a time
when my hand was my foot
and my foot was my hand

in utero
I was a fish
but there was nothing to do

so my fins grew
fingers and toes
thinking they might be of some use

and they grabbed the cord
rippled the waters
made babbles of bubbles

when I was born
toes and fingers clutched
bruised nipples
the chewy eiderdown

I wish that my hand was my foot
and my foot was my hand

I would pick up pencils with my toes
nibble hard skin from my sole

dive into a warm pool
without a splash

Love

I have grown to respect you
For years I took you for granted
And I was losing you

But now
Head to toe
I have grown into you

And as a token of my love
I forgive my nose
I forgive my gut
I forgive my lachrymose eyes

And lying in the bath
I like your imagination
My knee a turtle
My penis magnified

I like my hair greying
The moles on my skin
I like the still hard muscle of my thighs

I love you
And now
I don't want to lose you

Bone

on the verge of the road
the discreet white tent of the Scientific Unit
ripples in the wind

tests leading to feasible theories are being made
and a timeline would be useful

but the bone does not belong

back at the lab
the suspect femur is building a case
for a new tournure

feathered
dominant jaw
clawed like a heraldic beast

with luck there will be a shocking article in a journal

scientists are not ones for myths
certainly not amongst each other

but this
could be a fabulous moment

Ears

my ears are not my eyes
my ears are not shells
my ears are not peaches
my ears are not dishes

nor are they hairless
nor are they small
nor are they beautiful on the outside

they are beautiful on the inside
they have a fixed abode
they are cartilage hooks for pencils and cigarettes
they are something I would like to pass on

my ears are smooth like a baby's bum
my ears follow the stars
my ears are cultivating pearls

my ears are bats
they blink
open
and shut

Tortoise
for my grand-children

the skin that I'm in
is hard
hoary like a tortoise

a kagoul is my shell

working in all weathers
there is always more to do

stones that gather
like scathed children
weeds
that nothing will kill

I slowly munch through the roots
dig through dirt
to the bone

the skin that I'm in
is a carapace of keratin
that I've grown into

my hooded head
perfectly self contained

in a hundred years
though giant
I may be forgotten

but scrape your knees
and you shall know me

I Should Have Been Taller

but my duodenum would not allow it

my father was six foot two
my uncle too
but small for my size
only my large feet kept me from blowing over

so I looked up to others
concluded that it would be a small world
and regulated my bile
with milk
absorbed myself in those around me

I should have been taller
but I do not let it bother me

my digestion of the bitter pill
is so much better

Little Weed

my parents were easily embarrassed
as ambitious people often are

and did not want a weed for a child

so when my head
lost its crown of petals
I lay awake
and dreamed of horses and clocks

my father told me not to worry about such things
and bought me boxing gloves

my mother gave me a glass of water
and rubbed my back

I was wilted
wetting my bed
stressed by conditions undiagnosed

and supposed
that with a hollow stem for a spine
my chances of making it through the winter
were small
and I would die the slow death of an acolyte

but each year I return

with a head like a dandelion
and the tenacious root
that shouts
"I am alive!"

My Heart

has no enthusiasm for declarations of love
songs plucked from a lute are complex miscalculations

my heart has a job to do
and fit to the task
pumps the blood around my body

an iron ship upon the sea
it is a multi-chambered engine
that quickens to the action

my heart kills
all known contagions

my heart is
the simplest of equations

my heart has its reasons

why would you require more of my heart?

The Slim Shape

my mother was 36 24 36

I did not know what this meant
when I pushed in
the pointy tip of her bra
and watched it pop out again

it made me laugh
it made her laugh too

I like the boyish figure
slim hipped
not much of an arse

but I can never share my heart with those
whose clothes
take a straight line and hold to it

mother was a flirt
who married young
then thought better of it

but her round laugh
her round singsong head
was my first and only love

when the slim shape came in
she gave up and faded away at the edges

my mother was 36 24 36

but she
was without measure

Breathe

my mother lies
in a hospital in Cape Town

she is weak
and the doctor has yet to decide
what to do

she was found on the beach
confused
short of breath

they have found tangles in her brain
and there will be changes
and I must be strong

my mother lies
in a hospital in Cape Town
tells everyone that the country's gone to the dogs
since the blacks took over

when I rang
she asked if she was going mad

I did not tell her
she was sedated
with an anti-psychotic drug

so we talked about the rain

in this waiting game of telephone calls
the truth
is only the first casualty

my mother lies
in a hospital in Cape Town
her breathing though shallow now regular

and I am grateful
and shall not give in
to her small destructions of character

for I know
that as she breathes
so do I

and tomorrow
I must fly
to bring her home again

String
for my mother

my forehead
            has become clueless
I can't tell a
      bird from a banjo

but still
  I stand
            on my own
two
 feet
like an island of salt
        in a green field of dunnocks

sworn enemy
        of of the yellow thistle
  crows
  tarry a while
        rest their beaks
    upon my shoulder

my head
    cannot
        hold
        a clue

I could have sworn
I was in a red field of buttercups
a nut tree
    the throat of a nightingale

but still I stand

the moon
    heavy
  like a medicine ball

and I can't tell a bird from a banjo
                      a banjo
   from a ball

tarry
rest a while

  sing me
      a sad sad song

and you can have
      my ball of string

Elbow

below the humerus
the funny bone

a stupid place to put a nerve
trapped between the bone and the skin

the mighty greasy hinge
that creaks
after a certain age

until diagnosed as tennis elbow
even though you never picked up a racket

the hawser joint
not bendy
like the ball and socket of the shoulder

but a lusty link
to the delicate business of the hand and fingers

elbow
you have your own humdrum function
like the bowel

but without you
I couldn't cut my bread or itch my nose

and there's nothing funny about that

Song Of The Hips
after Lucille Clifton

my hips are ships

my hips are strong / my hips are wide
my hips follow the tide

my hips are mighty hips
I am captain of these hips

my hips have a jolly crew
my hips fly the red / white and blue

my hips hold precious cargo / my hips have tattoos

my hips are ropes / my hips are sails
my hips have a mermaid on their prow

when seas are rough / my hips come around

my hips weigh anchor / my hips bear true
my hips are meant for you

ahoy! / my hips! / they are ships!

Gut Flora

to breast milk and intestinal mucosa
we give thanks

for each baby blooming with bacteria
we give thanks

a florist would charge an arm and a leg
for such a bouquet

we give thanks for spores
for the way
that each part of the body tidies
up after itself

and working like a smooth semiotic machine
the great intestinal gardener
gathers muck into the magic chamber of the bowel

which we treasure
to bring forth night soil
and flowers
from the effort of our daily toil

without the flora of our guts
we would be
idle
too fatigued to raise our finger for a cuppa
to eat our supper

we would slowly waste away

for each protozoa
we give thanks

between parasite and host
there is always
a symbiotic relationship

so we pray
that forever there shall be
digestive harmony

a signifier
between good health
and catastrophe

Woman in her Bath
(1)

in the steamy smudge of mirror
you are thinking
there is too much solid flesh

but your belly is taut
(though it does not care for you)

the water chasing down your head
jets from your elbows
cracks the muscle of your breasts

casting upon the waters
the carnal debris of a shipwreck
your old substantive self

rising from the tub
you are thinking
about the baths you shared with your brother

with delicacy
you find the hard shadow of your rib

there is so much solid flesh
that to lose one self is no disaster
and always there is the salvation of water

(2)

you kneel in the bath
the head of the shower
like an umbrella

when the factory took
the water from the river
the tap dripped

and little brown fish swam
in your hair
and slid between your buttocks

you wipe the soap from your eyes
but do not like me
staring at you

with a hard syllabic look
you kick the door
back into the frame

Vertebrae

the spine
is the stave, upon which the body is composed

when you abandon
your dress (con brio)

I count the vertebrae
from C1 to L5

within your spine
there are sweet arpeggios, sonorous chords

I could play
a well tempered clavier
upon those bones
from prelude to a rousing fugue

the spine
the metrical line of beauty that harmonises the body

Dental

teeth
why bother?

a total clearance would save on the bills
make an ideal wedding present

the bride and groom slipping out of their teeth
and between the sheets

there are too many teeth in the world
grinning their way through a steak
chewing on pencils

maybe they are macerating stars
in the inky throat of the night
pearly sentinels to the gums

a right hook
would sort out the boys from the men

and in the long run
do you a favour as you peel back your dentures
like sardines in a tin

teeth
why bother?
and how are two eyes better than one?

and what say you about the tongue?

Hand

You feel like a plastic hand

Remote controlled

Taking your sweet time
To pick up a pen

We should be

Sequential

But I don't know
What you're going to do next

The night was long

When I woke up
My sense of you had gone

So Brother
Where have you been
And what can you tell me about it

The Claw

my father didn't live long enough
for the curse of arthritis
to bend him

a claw would have suited him

he could have scared his grand-children
to death
or until they wet themselves

that was him
and no better for it

but he had been misshapen
by bad luck
and sudden storms that broke upon him

I would have thought
a claw
a fine articulation

to catch and hold
the words
we could have spoken

but
in the ankylotic fusion
of my hand
lies
the salutary determinate of the man

something
which I cannot clasp
nor crush

Nose

nosebleeds
are rarely fatal

but the cascade of blood
upon
bad news
or a change in the weather

is strange phenomena
consociated with the iconography of saints

who emerge stigmatised from the bellies of dragons
carrying a large fish
which they devour with onions

the nose
the cavity of the sensitive soul
a refuge
from the blunt trauma of life

maybe a bridge
between us and the fine aquiline profile
of God

so when you sneeze blood
take care

you might be sneezing nails and thorns
the charismatic rapture
of old time religion

the arousal of the amygdala
is all very well

miracles take a little longer

Ode To The Spleen

my spleen has enlarged
taking over the function of the heart

my spleen thuds
with the blood of ill humour

like a wasps nest hanging by a petiole
my spleen chews
capriciousness into poison

a reservoir of melancholy
my spleen burns
to exudate the blood
flood each vascular organ

my spleen withers
like a grape on the vine
the cup of death is the sweetest wine

Procedure

as a rule
we should always tell the truth

the truth wants to confess
get everything off its chest

and bold without fear
or favour
the truth tells it like it is

when it smiles
the truth has dazzling perfect teeth

the truth loves to chew the fat

but as surgical intervention
can give the face
a loving re-invention

so the truth has wrinkles
that must be smoothed away

truth
is the art of construction

an ugly companion
that likes too much
the sound of its own voice

yet there is a beauty to truth
that lies
in the serpentine curve of expression
and that
is its fatal attraction

as a rule
we should always tell the truth

but breaking the rules
is the one true temptation

Axilla

do not shave your armpit

or spray
what makes you

your armpit
is a crab
hiding in a shell

a cat
happy in its hairy skin

like a wick
the hair of your axilla
soaks up sweat

sweet is the odour
of intertrigo

like tobacco
I inhale you

do not shave your armpit

Ambidextrous

                                        it's my right hand
                        that gets up to all the trouble

the left is a good lad

who you could trust with your money
or your wife

                              the right can catch a ball
                                    throw a punch
                                            a knife

the left
lacks strength and co-ordination

                                            the right
                                        is sinister
                                    in its motivation

                    there are times
         when left and right must work together
                  for the greater good

                  to hammer in a nail
                        lift a box
                       stack wood

                      like twins
                    there is love
              but left and right
          do not always get along

        there must be a dominant
                   and
            a subordinate one

Bones

between my father's bones
ash trees
root through thin soil

to the minerals
that lie in veins
above Aberystwyth

lead and gold
all matter of materials, that a man with a drill and a pick
could make a small living

and within my father's bones
long walks to faraway farmhouses
where sheep would eat anything

and inside my father's rib cage
the choir of the Sion Chapel, Vulcan Street
singing sweet and low

and between my father's toes
a stroll along the pier
and dancing with Betty and Pearl

and in my father's hands
the pulled feet of rabbits and crows

and within my father's ear
the whistle of the slow milk train to Paddington

and in my father's mouth
rwy'n dy garu di